The Story of a Special Day
Volume 62

March 2

61th day of the year
(62nd in leap years)
304 days remaining
until the end of the year.

by Michael Dobson

Timespinner
Press

Copyright Information

March 2: The Story of a Special Day (Vol. 62) is copyright © and trademarked ™ 2012 by Timespinner Press. All rights reserved. The Timespinner Press logo is trademarked by Timespinner Press.

For more information about the series, about me, or about your special day, please email us at editor@timespinnerpress.com.

Table of Contents

Cover: Detail from the flag of the Republic of Texas, celebrating Texas Independence Day

March 2 Quotations

"God did not create a human family made up of segregated, dissociated, mutually independent members. No; he would have them all united by the bond of total love of Him and consequent self-dedication to assisting each other to maintain that bond intact."

— Pope Pius XIII, born March 2, 1876

"From there to here/from here to there/funny things are everywhere."

— Theodor Seuss Geisel (Dr. Seuss), born March 2, 1904

"If what you have done yesterday still looks big to you, you haven't done much today."

— Mikhail Gorbachev, born March 2, 1931

"Reality is that which, when you stop believing in it, doesn't go away."

— Philip K. Dick, died March 2, 1982

Texas Independence Day

Texas Independence Day marks the anniversary of the adoption of the Texas Declaration of Independence on March 2, 1836. In that document, settlers from the United States who had taken up residence in Texas declared their independence from Mexico and established the Republic of Texas.

Spanish Texas had originally permitted colonists from the United States to settle in its territory, beginning with Stephen Austin's settlement of 1823. Mexico itself was newly independent from Spain, and suffered from political and economic instability. When General Antonio López de Santa Anna suspended the 1824 Mexican Constitution, civil war spread across the country.

Texas's first attempt to gain independence from Mexico resulted in the brief establishment of the Republic of Fredonia. The United States government, interested in the territory, offered to purchase Texas from Mexico for the sum of $1 million, but was refused.

3

Civil war broke out again in 1835. In February 1836 Santa Anna's forces laid siege to the Alamo, a small fort in San Antonio.

On March 2, Texas declared independence, and war was declared. On March 6, the Battle of the Alamo was won by the Mexican Army, but motivated the Texians to take revenge. On April 21, 1836, the Texian Army defeated Santa Anna at the Battle of San Jacinto, effectively ending Mexican control of Texas. Texas independence became official on May 14, 1836.

The Fall of the Alamo, by Robert Jenkins Onderdonk

March 2 Holidays and Celebrations

Victory at Adwa Day (Ethiopia)

Victory at Adwa Day celebrates the Ethiopian victory in climactic battle of the First Italo-Ethiopian War on March 1-2, 1896, securing Ethiopian sovereignty.

Ethiopian painting of the Battle of Adwa

Peasants Day (Burma)

Peasants Day in Burma marks the successful March 2, 1962, *coup d'etat* by Ne Win, who founded the Burma Socialist Programme Party and kept power until 1988.

Omizu-Okuri Festival (Obama, Japan)

The Japanese town of Obama, recently famous because of the name shared with the US President, celebrates the annual Water-Carrying Festival, in which water from the Onyu River is presented to the temple in a tradition dating back more than 1,200 years.

Feast of 'Alá (Bahá'í)

The first day of the 19th month of the Bahá'í calendar is the Feast of 'Alá (Loftiness), which begins the Nineteen Day Fast (see March Events).

Christian Feast Days

Saints commemorated on March 2 include Agnes of Bohemia; Blessed Charles the Good, Count of Flanders; and Chad of Mercia (Church of England).

What Happened on March 2?

1476 CE - Battle of Grandson

On March 2, 1476, a Swiss army defeated Charles the Bold, Duke of Burgundy, at the castle of Grandson, capturing the castle and a huge store of treasure, only to find over 400 Swiss prisoners that Charles had hanged several days earlier. This atrocity by Charles unified the Swiss, who annihilated the Burgundian army at the Battle of Murten in June of the same year.

1776 CE - Battle of the Rice Boats

On March 2-3, 1776, during the American Revolutionary War, Patriot militia from Georgia and South Carolina fought to prevent a British fleet from transporting rice and other supplies to the besieged British army in Boston. Although the battle failed to prevent the British from obtaining the necessary supplies, it did mark the end of British control of Georgia.

1808 CE - Legal Slave Importation Ended in the United States

On March 2, 1808, President Thomas Jefferson signed the Act Prohibiting Importation of Slaves, forbidding the importation of new slaves into the United States. Although the Act was not always well enforced, it was part of the general trend led by Great Britain to abolish the slave trade. Legal slavery in the US continued until the adoption of the 13th Amendment in 1865.

1825 CE - Capture of "El Pirata Cofresí"

On March 2, 1825, Roberto Cofresí, the most renowned pirate in Puerto Rico, along with eleven members of his pirate crew, was captured by Captain John D. Sloat, commander of the US schooner *Grampus*. The pirates were tried before a Spanish military court, convicted, and executed by firing squad on March 29, 1825.

1877 CE - Congress Elects Rutherford B. Hayes

Although presidential candidate Samuel J. Tilden received 184 electoral votes (and more than 50% of the popular vote) to Rutherford B. Hayes's 165 votes, there were 20 electoral votes in dispute, in which each party reported their candidate had won the state. A bitter legal and political battle resulted in the appointment of a 15 member Electoral Commission to settle the matter. They elected Hayes as president, under a deal known as the Compromise of 1877, which ended Reconstruction in the South.

1919 CE - **Comintern Founded**

The first international congress of the Communist Party met in Moscow, site of the successful Bolshevik Revolution of 1917. Communist delegates from 34 nations attended.

1933 CE - *King Kong* **Premiers**

On March 2, 1933, lines formed around the block for the Radio City Music Hall premier of the new monster movie *King Kong*. The movie played in two theaters: the 6,200-seat music hall itself, and the 3,700-seat RKO Roxy across the street. Tickets were priced at a premium-priced 35¢ ($6.20 today) to 75¢ ($13.29), when movies generally cost a nickel. Every show was sold out for four consecutive days, setting an all-time attendance record for an indoor event.

Original theatrical poster for *King Kong*

1946 CE - *Lucky Lady II* Circles the Globe

The *Lucky Lady II*, a Boeing B-50 Superfortress, became the first airplane to circle the world nonstop, using in-flight refueling to stay aloft for 94 hours and 1 minute. It took off from Fort Worth, Texas, on February 26, 1946, and landed March 2. The fuselage of the plane is at the Planes of Fame Museum in Chino, California.

1962 CE - Wilt Chamberlain's 100 Point Game

On March 2, 1962, basketball star Wilt Chamberlain set the single-game scoring record in the NBA by scoring 100 points for the Philadelphia Warriors against the New York Knicks. The final score was 169-147. Chamberlain's achievement broke his own record of 78 points scored in a single game.

1972 CE - Pioneer 10 Launched

NASA's Pioneer 10 space probe, launched March 2, 1972, from Cape Canaveral, Florida, was the first spacecraft to cross the asteroid belt, the first spacecraft to reach Jupiter, and the first spacecraft to achieve escape velocity from the solar system. Communication with the satellite was lost January 23, 2003.

Pioneer 10

1993 CE - Storm of the Century

The 1993 superstorm known as the "Storm of the Century" formed over the Gulf of Mexico on March 2, 1993, and dissipated two weeks later. It stretched from Canada to Central America, with snows of up to 12 inches in such places as Birmingham, Alabama, and the Florida Panhandle. It caused power outages for more than 10 million people and killed 310.

Satellite image of the 1993 Storm of the Century

Who Was Born on March 2?

The abbreviation "O.S." on some dates refers to the fact that the Russian Empire did not switch from the Julian to the Gregorian calendar at the same time as the rest of Europe, and therefore some figures have two dates for their birth or death.

People whose original names are not in the Western alphabet have their native names in the appropriate script shown in parenthesis.

Art and Literature

Peter Straub (March 2, 1943 —)

Award-winning horror writer Peter Straub's *Ghost Story* was adapted into a movie starring Fred Astaire.

John Irving (March 2, 1942 —)

Novelist John Irving wrote *The World According to Garp, The Cider House Rules,* and *A Prayer for Owen Meany,* among others. He received an Academy Award for Best Adapted Screenplay for his adaption of *The Cider House Rules.*

Tom Wolfe (March 2, 1931 —)

Tom Wolfe began as a leader of the New Journalism literary movement with *The Electric Kool-Aid Acid Test,* and went on to write such books as *The Right Stuff* and *The Bonfire of the Vanities.*

Theodor Seuss Geisel (Dr. Seuss) (March 2, 1904 — September 24, 1991)

Writer, poet, and cartoonist Theodor Seuss Geisel is best known for his children's books written under the name of Dr. Seuss. He first became famous for his advertisements for the insecticide Flit, and wrote *Private Snafu* films for the Army during World War II.

Theodor Seuss Geisel

Sholem Aleichem (שלום־עליכם) (March 2 [O.S. February 18], 1859 — May 13, 1916)

Yiddish author Sholem Aleichem is best known for his stories about Tevye the Milkman, which were adapted as the musical *Fiddler on the Roof.*

Movies and Television

Daniel Craig (March 2, 1968 —)

Actor Daniel Craig became the sixth actor to play the role of James Bond in 2006's *Casino Royale*. Other notable movie roles included *The Golden Compass* and *Cowboys and Aliens*.

Gates McFadden (March 2, 1949 —)

Gates McFadden is best known for playing Dr. Beverly Crusher in the television and movie series *Star Trek: The Next Generation*.

Jennifer Jones (March 2, 1919 — December 17, 2009)

Jennifer Jones won the Academy Award for Best Actress for her role in 1943's *The Song of Bernadette*.

Desi Arnaz (March 2, 1917 — December 2, 1968)

Cuban band leader Desi Arnaz became famous for his role as Ricky Ricardo on the television series *I Love Lucy*, and is credited as the inventor of the rerun.

Desi Arnaz

Willis O'Brien (March 2, 1886 — November 8, 1962)

Movie special effects pioneer Willis O'Brien's stop-motion animation work was featured in numerous movies, including 1933's *King Kong*.

Music

Jon Bon Jovi (March 2, 1962 —)

Musician Jon Bon Jovi founded the eponymous rock band Bon Jovi and served as lead singer. He was inducted into the Songwriters Hall of Fame in 2009.

Karen Carpenter (March 2, 1950 — February 4, 1983)

Drummer and singer Karen Carpenter and her brother Richard formed The Carpenters music group. She suffered from anorexia and died of heart failure related to her illness at the age of 32.

Lou Reed (March 2, 1942 —)

Singer and songwriter Lou Reed came to fame as leader of The Velvet Underground and went on to a successful solo career beginning with his 1971 hit, "Walk on the Wild Side."

Kurt Weill (March 2, 1900 — April 3, 1950)

Composer and playwright Kurt Weill is best known for *The Threepenny Opera,* which gave rise to the hit song "Mack the Knife."

Bedřich Smetana (March 2, 1824 — May 12, 1884)

Czech composer Bedřich Smetana is best known for his opera *The Bartered Bride.*

Politics and Law

Shoko Asahara (麻原 彰晃) (March 2, 1955 —)

Shoko Asahara founded the Japanese religious group Aum Shinrikyo, which under his leadership committed the 1995 sarin gas attack on the Tokyo subway.

Russ Feingold (March 2, 1953 —)

Russ Feingold was a United States Senator from Wisconsin from 1993 to 2011, known for co-sponsorship of the McCain-Feingold campaign finance reform legislation. He received the John F. Kennedy Profile in Courage Award.

Mikhail Gorbachev (Михаил Горбачёв) (March 2, 1931 —)

As General Secretary of the Communist Party of the Soviet Union, Mikhail Gorbachev presided over the dissolution of the Soviet Union in 1991. He received the Nobel Peace Prize in 1990.

Robert H. Michel (March 2, 1923 —)

Illinois congressman Robert H. Michel served as Minority Leader of the US House of Representatives for 14 years and as Minority Whip for 6 years.

Sam Houston (March 2, 1793 — July 26, 1863)

Sam Houston played a leading role in bringing Texas into the United States. The city of Houston is named for him.

DeWitt Clinton (March 2, 1769 — February 11, 1828)

US Senator and Governor of New York, DeWitt Clinton was largely responsible for the construction of the Erie Canal.

Religion

Pope Pius XII (March 2, 1876 — October 9, 1959)

Pius XII was elevated to the papacy on his birthday, March 2, 1939. His leadership of the Catholic Church during World War II remains a subject of controversy.

Science and Technology

Edward Condon (March 2, 1902— March 26, 1974)

Nuclear physicist Edward Condon was part of the Manhattan Project to build the atomic bomb. He became known publicly for his 1968 *Condon Report,* an official USAF study that debunked UFO sightings as a variety of natural phenomena.

Sports

Reggie Bush (March 2, 1985 —)

NFL Miami Dolphins running back Reggie Bush won the Heisman Trophy in 2005, but relinquished it following an NCAA investigation of the USC football program involving improper benefits.

Hayley Lewis (March 2, 1974 —)

Swimmer Hayley Lewis won five gold and one bronze medal at the 1990 Commonwealth Games, and a silver medal in the 1992 Olympics. She hosted the Australian version of the television show *The Biggest Loser.*

Denny Crum (March 2, 1937 —)

University of Louisville men's basketball coach Denny Crum was elected to the Naismith Memorial Basketball Hall of Fame in 1994.

Cal Abrams (March 2, 1924 — February 25, 1997)

Cal Abrams played for the Brooklyn Dodgers from 1949 to 1952, and for Cincinnati, Pittsburgh, Baltimore, and Chicago until 1956, a total of 567 major league games.

Jim Konstanty (March 2, 1917 — June 11, 1976)

Baseball relief pitcher Jim Konstanty was named the National League MVP of 1950. As a pitcher, he achieved 268 career strikeouts.

Mort Cooper (March 2, 1913 — November 17, 1958)

Pitcher Mort Cooper was named the National League Most Valuable Player of 1942. As a pitcher, he achieved 913 career strikeouts.

Mel Ott (March 2, 1909 — November 21, 1958)

New York Giant Mel Ott was the first National League player to score 500 home runs.

Mel Ott

Moe Berg (March 2, 1902 — May 29, 1972

Major league baseball catcher and coach Moe Berg was known as "the brainiest guy in baseball," and served as a spy with the OSS during World War II.

Who Died on March 2?

Acting

Randolph Scott

Randolph Scott (January 23, 1898 — March 2, 1987)

Leading man Randolph Scott appeared in numerous genre films, but is best remembered for his roles as a Western hero.

Eric Blore (December 23, 1887 — March 2, 1959)

Known for his performances as a stuffy butler, Eric Blore appeared in many of the Fred Astaire and Ginger Rogers musicals for RKO.

Literature

Philip K. Dick (December 16, 1928 — March 2, 1982)

Science fiction author Philip K. Dick published 44 novels. Although he spent most of his career in near-poverty, ten highly successful films have been made based on his books, including *Blade Runner* (based on *Do Androids Dream of Electric Sheep?)* and *Total Recall* (based on *We Can Remember It For You Wholesale).*

D. H. Lawrence (September 11, 1885 — March 2, 1930)

Although D. H. Lawrence wrote many books, he is best remembered for his controversial bestseller *Lady Chatterley's Lover,* widely condemned as pornographic in its time, but considered an enduring classic of modernist literature today.

Horace Walpole (September 24, 1717 — March 2, 1797)

Horace Walpole, 4th Earl of Oxford, is remembered for his home Strawberry Hill in Twickenham, and for his Gothic novel *The Castle of Otranto*.

Religion

John Wesley

John Wesley (June 28 [O.S. June 17], 1703 — March 2, 1791)

Theologian and evangelist John Wesley founded the Methodist movement. His teachings are also influential in the Holiness movement, Pentecostalism, and the Charismatic and Neo-Charismatic movements.

Sports

Fred Merkle (December 20, 1888 — March 2, 1956)

First baseman Fred Merkle's lengthy career in baseball was overshadowed by a baserunning mistake in his youth, known as "Merkle's boner."

Fred Merkle

The month of March, from the illuminated manuscript
Les Très Riches Heures du duc de Berry

March: The Story of a Month

The Third Month

In ancient Rome, March was the first month of the year. As the first month of spring, in the Mediterranean climate it marked the beginning of the military campaign season. That's why March (Martius) is named in honor of Mars, the Roman god of war.

Although the first month of the year was moved back to January sometime during the transition of Rome from a kingdom to a republic (historians differ), March was the first month of the year in Russia until the end of the 15th Century, and is the first month of the year in many other cultures and religions.

In the northern hemisphere, March 1 marks the beginning of meteorological spring. In the southern hemisphere, March is the equivalent of

September, making southern hemisphere March the beginning of autumn.

March is one of the seven months that have 31 days in it. March starts on the same day of the week as November every year, and except for leap years starts on the same day as February. March starts on the same day of the week as the previous June except for leap years, and in leap years starts on the same day as the previous September and December.

March in Other Cultures

In Finland, March is called *maaliskuu* (earthy month). In Ukraine, it's *березень* (birch tree). Other names for March include *Lentmonat* (Saxon), *Hyld-monath* (Angles), and *sušec* (Slovene).

March Symbols

Birthstones: Aquamarine and bloodstone, both representing courage.

Aquamarine

Birth Flowers Daffodils

Daffodils in Bagatelle Park, Paris, France

March Events

Honorary months: Presidents, Congresses, and nations around the world issue proclamations recognizing particular months to honor certain causes. These events generally fall in March. (All US unless otherwise noted.)

- National Nutrition Month

- American Red Cross Month

- Women's History Month (celebrated in Canada during October)

- Irish-American Heritage Month

- Colorectal Cancer Awareness Month

- Fire Prevention Month (The Philippines)

Women's Suffrage picket line, 1917

"March Madness": (United States) The NCAA Men's Division I Basketball Championship, popularly known as "March Madness" or the "Big Dance," is a single-elimination tournament to establish the champion college basketball team.

Multi-day events: Some March events span multiple days.

- **Nineteen Day Fast:** (Bahá'í Faith) March 2 through March 20

Movable events: Some events change dates from year to year.

- **Mardi Gras:** French for "Fat Tuesday," this celebration takes place the day before Ash Wednesday, the beginning of the Lenten season. The New Orleans Mardi Gras celebration is perhaps the most famous, but Mardi Gras and the Carnival season (between Ephiphany and Ash Wednesday) are celebrated in many areas with large Catholic populations. Mardi Gras can take place anywhere from February 3 to March 9 in regular years, and from February 4 to March 9 in leap years.

- **Casimir Pulaski Day:** (Illinois) The first Monday in March is observed as a holiday in Illinois, in memory of the Revolutionary War cavalry officer born in Poland. Dates range from March 1 to March 7.

Mardi Gras Night Parade, New Orleans, 2012

March Zodiac Signs

From the perspective of someone on Earth, the Sun appears to move through the sky throughout the year, along a path astronomers call the ecliptic plane. The ecliptic plane is divided into twelve constellations, known as the zodiac, based on traditionally observed patterns of stars. On your birthday, you can't see your constellation, because it's part of the daytime sky.

The zodiac was first developed by Babylonian astronomers about 2,500 years ago. Because they were unaware that the Earth wobbles like a spinning top (a motion known as *precession*), they didn't make allowance for the fact that the Sun's path through the zodiac changes over time.

That means there are now two sets of dates for your birth sign. The *tropical dates* are the original Babylonian dates; the *siderial dates* tell you where the Sun actually appears as it moves along its annual path.

Zodiac signs in March are Aquarius, Pisces, and Aries.

Aquarius

Tropical January 20 to February 19

Siderial February 12 to March 8 (March 9 in leap years)

Aquarius is one of the oldest recognized constellations, originally representing the Babylonian god Ea. In Latin, Aquarius means "water-carrier," represented in its symbol. In Greek mythology, Aquarius is sometimes associated with Deucalion, who survived a world-cleansing flood. In Chinese astronomy, it is known as the Black Tortoise of the North (北方玄武, Běi Fāng Xuán Wǔ).

In astrology, Aquarius is considered to be masculine and extroverted, and despite the name is an air sign. Aquarians are supposed to be philanthropical, inventive, and individualistic.

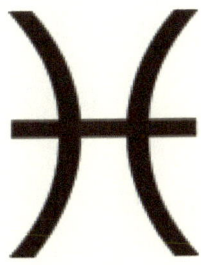

Pisces

Tropical February 20 to March 20

Siderial March 15 to April 14

In the Roman legend of Venus and her son Cupid, they escaped the clutches of Typhon, known as the "father of all monsters," by transforming into fish and tying themselves together with rope. That's why the name Pisces is plural for fish. The constellation appears as a somewhat ragged "V" shape, representing the rope, with the "fish" located at the two rope ends.

In astrology, Pisces is a water sign, compatible with the other water signs Cancer and Scorpio, as well as with the earth signs Taurus, Virgo, and Capricorn. Pisceans are supposed to be imaginative, compassionate, unworldly, secretive, and escapist.

What Day of the Week?

On what day of the week does March 2 fall?

Unfortunately, this isn't an easy question. Because the calendar year is 365 days long (366 in leap years), it doesn't divide evenly by the seven days of the week.

Also, the Earth goes around the Sun in about 365-1/4 days, so a calendar tends to drift over time. That's why the same date falls on different weekdays in different years.

This is made even more complicated by a change in calendars that took place in 1582. Our modern calendar has its roots in ancient Rome, in a calendar reform conducted by Julius Caesar. Caesar commissioned mathematicians to attack the problem, and came up with the idea of *leap years*, and thus standardized the calendar for centuries to come. This was called the *Julian calendar.*

Over time, however, the small errors in Caesar's calculation compounded. That's why Pope Gregory XIII commissioned the *Gregorian calendar*, used in most of the world today. Some countries converted in 1582, when the calendar was first developed; some converted later; other still haven't changed.

Gregorian and Julian aren't the only types of calendars. The Hebrew year, the Islamic year, and many other calendars are used in different parts of the world and among different people.

You can convert Gregorian dates to other calendars, including the Hebrew calendar, the Islamic calendar, and even the Mayan calendar by visiting the Fourmilab Calendar Converter at http://www.fourmilab.ch/documents/calendar/.

A 50-year brass perpetual calendar.

Copyright, Credit, and Contact

Follow Us

Our blog Dobson's Improbable History features short articles on events and people associated with each day, and updates several times each week. Get the latest on Twitter @SidewiseThinker.

Sources and Art Credits

Primary research source is Wikipedia, supplemented by other sources and personal research. All art and photographs are from Wikimedia Commons unless otherwise identified, and are either in the public domain or used under a Creative Commons license. Attribution is provided where requested by the copyright owner or when of historical significance, listed below.

- The flag of the Republic of Texas is in the public domain and is not an object of copyright.

- The painting *The Fall of the Alamo* by Robert Jenkins Onderdonk is in the public domain because its copyright has expired.

- The photograph of painting of the Battle of Adwa is in the public domain. The original painting is in the British Museum in London.

- The 1933 theatrical poster for *King Kong* is in the public domain because its copyright was not renewed.

- The photograph of Pioneer 10 and the satellite image of the 1993 Storm of the Century were created by NASA and are in the public domain.

- The photograph of Dr. Seuss (Theodor Seuss Geisel) was taken by Al Ravenna of the newspaper *World Telegram & Sun*. It is part of a collection donated to the Library of Congress by the newspaper, and all rights were dedicated to the public.

- The 1950 publicity photograph of Desi Arnaz was released by General Artists Corporation and is in the public domain.

- The 1986 photograph of Mikhail Gorbachev is from the Russian International News Agency, and is used under the Creative Commons Attribution-Share Alike 3.0 Unported License.

- The 1940 Bowman Gum baseball card of Mel Ott and the 1951 card of Jim Konstanty are the public domain because their copyrights were not renewed.

- The publicity photograph of Randolph Scott is in the public domain.

- The portrait of John Wesley is from the Library of Congress's Prints and Photographs Division. It is in the public domain because its copyright has expired.

- The American Tobacco Company baseball card of Fred Merkle is in the public domain because its copyright has expired.

- The illustration of the month of March is from the French Gothic illuminated manuscript *Les Très Riches Heures du duc de Berry* by the Limbourg Brothers, Jean Colombe, and an intermediate painter whose name is lost to history.

- The photograph of aquamarine has been released into the public domain.

- The photograph of daffodils is by Myrabella, and is licensed under the Creative Commons Attribution-Share Alike 3.0 Unported license.

- The 1917 Women's Suffrage demonstration comes from the Library of Congress, Prints and Photographs Division, LC-USZ62-31799 DLC

- The photograph of the 2012 Mardi Gras Night Parade was taken by Mills Baker, licensed under the Creative Commons Attribution 2.0 Generic License.

- The photograph of *hanácké kraslice*, a traditional way of decorating Easter eggs with straw, was taken on an exhibition of egg decorating in Bělkovice-Lašťany in the Czech Republic, and is in the public domain.

- The 50-year perpetual calendar photograph is in the public domain.

www.ingramcontent.com/pod-product-compliance
Lightning Source LLC
Chambersburg PA
CBHW050346290526
45785CB00006B/2652